A Night of Devastation: The Five Points South Mass Shooting in Birmingham

Abhirup Biswas

Disclaimer

This eBook, *"A Night of Devastation: The Five Points South Mass Shooting in Birmingham,"* is a nonfiction account based on publicly available information, reports, and witness statements concerning the events of September 21, 2024. While every effort has been made to ensure the accuracy of the information, details may change as the investigation progresses. This book is intended for educational and informational purposes only and should not be considered a comprehensive or final source on the event. The author is not liable for any actions taken based on the content of this eBook. The views expressed are those of the author and do not represent official statements from law enforcement, medical professionals, or legal entities involved. Readers are encouraged to seek official sources for updates.

The author and publisher accept no liability for any actions taken or not taken based on the contents of this eBook.

Preface

The night of September 21, 2024, changed Birmingham forever. What started as an ordinary Saturday evening in the bustling Five Points South district ended in horror, as a mass shooting claimed the lives of four innocent people and left at least 18 others wounded. The community was shaken to its core, grappling with grief, anger, and the painful reality that gun violence can strike anywhere, at any time.

This eBook was born out of the need to tell the stories of that night—not just the brutal facts of the crime but the human impact. It is a tribute to the victims who lost their lives, the survivors who must now heal both physically and emotionally, and the first responders who bravely ran toward danger to save others. It is also a reflection on the broader issue of gun violence that has plagued not only Birmingham but communities across the United States.

Through this book, I aim to honor those affected by this tragedy and shed light on the complex societal, cultural, and legal factors that make events like this possible. I hope that by understanding the full scope of what happened, we can come together as a society to address the root causes of violence and work toward creating a safer future for all.

This is not just the story of one terrible night in Birmingham—it is part of a much larger conversation about how we, as a community and a nation, respond to violence, support those who are grieving, and take action to prevent such horrors from repeating. In writing this book, I've drawn from official reports, witness accounts, and news coverage, but the story it tells is ultimately about more than facts and figures. It is about human lives, loss, resilience, and the enduring hope that we can do better.

Thank you for reading, and may we never forget the lives that were lost on that tragic night. Let their memory be the catalyst for change.

Table of Contents

Introduction: When Darkness Fell on Birmingham

Birmingham, Alabama—a city known for its rich history, southern charm, and vibrant culture—became the backdrop to unimaginable tragedy on the night of September 21st, 2024. It was a typical Saturday night in Five Points South, the heart of the city's nightlife, where laughter and music filled the air. However, in a matter of seconds, this joyful evening turned into a nightmare.

Gunfire erupted in the bustling district, turning a popular entertainment area into a war zone. Four people were brutally gunned down, and at least 18 others were left wounded—some fighting for their lives. It was a mass shooting that not only shook Birmingham to its core but also reverberated throughout the nation, reminding us yet again of the devastating impact of gun violence.

This eBook delves deep into that fateful night, examining the event in chilling detail. From the tragic stories of the victims to the bravery of first responders, we will explore the raw emotions and realities of those affected. But we will also look beyond the immediate tragedy to uncover the larger societal issues that enabled such violence to occur. This book is not just a recounting—it is a call to action.

Chapter 1: A City in Shock – The Night of Horror

1.1 A Vibrant Night Turns Deadly

Five Points South is no stranger to large crowds on the weekends. Known for its lively bars, eclectic restaurants, and bustling nightlife, it draws in a diverse array of people—from students at the nearby university to families enjoying a night out. On this particular Saturday night, the streets were alive with the buzz of activity. Music spilled out from bars, and people laughed as they waited in line to get into their favorite spots.

But just after 11 p.m., the scene changed in an instant. A group of people stood outside Hush, a hookah and cigar lounge on Magnolia Avenue, chatting and enjoying the evening air. Suddenly, a flurry of gunshots rang out. What had been a peaceful Saturday night was quickly transformed into a night of terror.

1.2 The Unleashing of Violence

Eyewitnesses reported seeing flashes of gunfire. Some described hearing rapid-fire bursts that sounded more like a military weapon than a civilian firearm. The shooters had unleashed violence on a group of innocent bystanders. The weapon was later identified as having been modified with a "Glock switch"—a device that turns a semi-automatic pistol into a fully automatic machine gun. The air was filled with the terrifying sound of bullets ricocheting off cars, shattering windows, and cutting down anyone in their path.

People screamed. They ducked for cover behind anything they could find—cars, trash bins, and storefronts. Some were struck by the bullets almost immediately, while others ran in sheer panic, trying to escape the deadly onslaught.

1.3 Immediate Panic and Chaos

For those who survived the initial gunfire, the world seemed to slow down. The once lively street was now a scene of carnage. People were lying on the ground, some motionless, others crying out in pain. Friends and strangers alike dragged wounded victims to safety, while others called 911, their hands shaking with fear.

The sheer scale of the attack was disorienting. Gunfire had sprayed across the busy avenue, hitting patrons standing outside several businesses. Witnesses said it felt like the bullets were coming from every direction, and no one could tell where the shooters were. Some believed it was a drive-by shooting, while others thought the gunmen had been on foot, slipping away into the shadows after committing their horrifying act.

Chapter 2: The Lives Lost – Remembering the Victims

2.1 Stories of the Innocent Victims

In the aftermath, the lives of four individuals were tragically cut short. Two men and a woman were found lying lifeless on the sidewalk by responding officers, their bodies unresponsive to any life-saving measures. A fourth man was rushed to UAB Hospital, where doctors fought to save him, but despite their best efforts, he too succumbed to his injuries.

These were not just faceless names in a tragic statistic—they were real people with dreams, aspirations, and loved ones. One of the victims, a local musician, had been known to frequent the area for inspiration. Another was a father of two, celebrating a friend's birthday on what was supposed to be a night of joy. Their families would forever remember that night, the hole it left in their lives impossible to fill.

2.2 The Families Left Behind

For the families of the victims, the news came like a tidal wave, crashing into their lives and sweeping away everything they knew. One mother described receiving the call about her son, feeling her legs give out beneath her as her world collapsed. The pain of losing a loved one to such senseless violence is immeasurable, and for these families, the night of September 21st would be forever etched into their hearts.

The families spoke of the unimaginable grief they now carry, the anguish of planning funerals instead of celebrating life milestones. "I never thought I'd bury my child," said one heartbroken parent. Another expressed disbelief, saying, "He was just out for a fun night—how could this happen?"

2.3 The Injured: Survivors' Road to Recovery

For the 18 others who survived the attack but were injured, the path to recovery is long and uncertain. Some remain in critical condition, battling for their lives in hospital rooms, while others, though stable, face months—if not years—of physical therapy and rehabilitation. The emotional scars run even deeper.

One young woman, hit in the leg by a stray bullet, recalls the horror of that night. "I still can't believe

I'm alive," she says, her voice trembling. "I can't sleep. Every time I close my eyes, I see the gun, I hear the screams. I don't know how to move on from this."

Chapter 3: Heroism Amidst the Chaos – The Immediate Response

3.1 First Responders' Brave Actions

The chaos that unfolded in the minutes after the shooting was met with remarkable bravery by Birmingham's first responders. South Precinct officers were the first on the scene, rushing into the danger without hesitation. They moved quickly to secure the area, searching for suspects while also rendering aid to the victims. Their calm under pressure helped prevent further injury, but the carnage they encountered was overwhelming.

"I've been a cop for over 20 years, and I've never seen anything like this," said one officer, his face lined with exhaustion and emotion. "There were bodies everywhere. People were screaming for help, and we had to push past that panic to do our jobs."

3.2 Firefighters and Medics: Saving Lives in the Line of Duty

As police worked to secure the scene, Birmingham Fire and Rescue teams arrived to provide emergency medical care. Firefighters and paramedics were vital in stabilizing the wounded, rushing them to local hospitals. With over a dozen critically injured, they worked against the clock, every second counting in their effort to save lives.

Their quick thinking saved many from death. "They're heroes," said a survivor who had been shot in the abdomen. "I wouldn't be here without them. They showed up and got me out of there when I thought I was going to die."

3.3 Police Response: Securing the Scene and Calming the Crowd

As news of the shooting spread, more and more officers descended upon Five Points South. With the streets still filled with terrified patrons, law enforcement quickly set up a massive perimeter, blocking off streets and ensuring no further attacks occurred. Officers had to manage the crowd, both calming those who had witnessed the shooting and ensuring that no evidence was lost in the ensuing chaos.

The scene was chaotic, with hundreds of people gathering to see what had happened. Some came looking for loved ones, while others, drawn by morbid curiosity, tried to get closer to the crime scene. Police officers worked tirelessly to maintain order while detectives began their investigation.

Chapter 4: Investigating a Tragedy – Law Enforcement and Evidence Gathering

4.1 The Initial Investigation: Unraveling the Scene

Investigating a mass shooting is no easy task, and the detectives tasked with piecing together what happened at Five Points South had an enormous challenge ahead of them. Officers initially had to focus on two things: caring for the victims and ensuring no suspects escaped the area. Detectives began combing through the crime scene almost immediately, searching for clues, ballistics evidence, and any signs that could help identify the perpetrators.

The Five Points area is known for its many security cameras, which proved vital in the investigation. Detectives collected hours of footage from businesses along Magnolia Avenue, hoping to catch a glimpse of the shooters. Witnesses were interviewed, though many were in shock and unable to provide clear details.

4.2 Working with Federal Agencies: ATF and FBI's Role

As the scale of the tragedy became apparent, local law enforcement reached out to federal partners for assistance. The ATF (Bureau of Alcohol, Tobacco, Firearms, and Explosives) and the FBI joined the investigation, bringing in specialized resources to track down the source of the weaponry used. The Glock switch, a device used to modify the gun into a fully automatic weapon, became a central focus.

Federal agents worked closely with Birmingham police, analyzing ballistics and tracking any potential leads related to the illegal modification of firearms. Given the widespread problem of modified weapons in urban areas, the FBI and ATF were already familiar with the issue and mobilized quickly to assist.

4.3 Hunting the Perpetrators: The Ongoing Investigation

Despite the massive law enforcement presence, no arrests were made in the immediate aftermath of the shooting. The investigation continued, with officers pursuing every possible lead. The lack of clear suspects left the city on edge, wondering when or if the perpetrators would be caught.

Police made public appeals for help, urging anyone with information, no matter how small, to come forward. "There's no detail too insignificant," said Officer Truman Fitzgerald during a press conference. "We are committed to finding out who did this and bringing them to justice."

Chapter 5: The Weapon of Destruction – The Role of the Glock Switch

5.1 A Weapon of War: Understanding the Glock Switch

The gunfire that erupted in Five Points South was no ordinary burst of shots—it was the kind of sustained, rapid firing usually heard in war zones. The reason for this terrifying sound was the use of a Glock switch, a small device that turns a standard semi-automatic pistol into a fully automatic weapon, capable of firing multiple bullets in a matter of seconds.

The device is illegal under federal law, but it has become increasingly common in cities across the United States. With just a simple modification, a gun that typically fires one round per trigger pull can now unleash an entire magazine in the blink of an eye. For law enforcement, it is one of the most dangerous tools in circulation, as it turns even basic firearms into weapons of mass destruction.

5.2 How the Glock Switch Exacerbates the Threat

In the case of the Birmingham shooting, witnesses described the sound of the gunfire as relentless, a terrifying barrage of bullets that seemed to last forever. This type of shooting makes it nearly impossible for people to find cover or flee before they are struck. The shooters at Five Points South used the switch to maximize damage, spraying bullets indiscriminately into a crowd.

The Glock switch doesn't just make the weapon more deadly—it makes it harder for law enforcement to respond. The overwhelming firepower gives shooters the advantage, allowing them to inflict massive casualties before police can react.

5.3 Legislative Battles: The Struggle to Control Modified Firearms

Lawmakers in Alabama, and across the country, have been trying to pass legislation to control the sale and possession of Glock switches. In Alabama, Representative Phillip Ensler has introduced legislation making it a Class C felony to possess or sell one of these devices, which could carry a sentence of up to 10 years in prison.

However, efforts to ban these devices face significant opposition. Gun rights advocates argue that the focus should be on the criminals who misuse the guns, rather than on the devices themselves. Meanwhile, the rising tide of gun violence in cities like Birmingham only makes the need for stricter controls more urgent.

Chapter 6: A City Under Siege – Birmingham's Gun Violence Crisis

6.1 Gun Violence Statistics in Birmingham: A Sobering Look

The mass shooting in Five Points South was not an isolated incident in Birmingham. In fact, it was part of a disturbing trend that has gripped the city in recent years. Birmingham, like many cities across America, has seen a rise in gun-related homicides, with 2024 already proving to be a particularly deadly year.

Before the Five Points shooting, Birmingham had recorded 118 homicides, and the death toll now stands at 122. Jefferson County, which includes Birmingham, had 154 homicides. These numbers paint a grim picture of a city under siege, where arguments are often settled with bullets rather than words.

6.2 Mass Shootings in the Context of Broader Violence

The tragedy at Five Points South is part of a larger pattern of mass shootings plaguing the nation. In Birmingham alone, there have been two other quadruple homicides this year. One occurred in July, when four people were killed in a drive-by shooting at an adult birthday party. Another took place in February, when four men were killed in a similar drive-by attack.

These mass shootings are not just statistics—they are the result of a complex web of social, economic, and cultural factors that drive individuals to commit such heinous acts. Poverty, systemic inequality, the easy access to firearms, and a culture that often glorifies violence all contribute to the rising tide of gun violence in Birmingham.

6.3 Why Birmingham? Cultural, Economic, and Social Roots of the Crisis

Birmingham has long struggled with issues of inequality and poverty, both of which feed into the cycle of violence. In many of the city's poorest neighborhoods, young people grow up with limited access to education, employment opportunities, and mental health resources. Guns often become the tool of choice for settling disputes, and the proliferation of firearms in the community only makes these conflicts more deadly.

Cultural factors also play a role. As Officer Truman Fitzgerald put it, "We're seeing far too many arguments being settled by bullets." This shift in how conflicts are resolved points to a deeper cultural problem—one that must be addressed if the city is to have any hope of stemming the tide of violence.

Chapter 7: The Search for Justice

7.1 The Difficulty of Bringing Perpetrators to Justice

As of the writing of this eBook, no arrests have been made in the Five Points South shooting. The search for those responsible continues, but the investigation is complex and time-consuming. In cases like this, where multiple shooters are involved and evidence is scattered, finding the culprits can be a daunting task for law enforcement.

7.2 The Role of Surveillance: Cameras and Witness Testimonies

One of the key tools in the investigation has been the surveillance cameras placed throughout the Five Points area. Detectives have poured over hours of footage, hoping to identify the shooters or their getaway vehicle. While the cameras provide crucial evidence, they cannot tell the whole story. That's why police have urged anyone with information—no matter how small—to come forward.

Witness testimonies are often crucial in these cases, but they can also be unreliable. In the chaos of the shooting, many witnesses were in shock, and their recollections may be hazy. Still, detectives are piecing together every bit of evidence they can to track down those responsible.

7.3 The Community's Call for Action

In the aftermath of the shooting, the Birmingham community has been vocal in its call for justice. Vigils were held to honor the victims, with hundreds gathering to pay their respects. Community leaders have called for a renewed effort to curb gun violence in the city, urging lawmakers to pass stricter gun control measures and increase funding for mental health and social services.

"There's something deeply broken when a night out with friends can end in death," said one local pastor during a vigil. "We need to do more than just mourn—we need to demand change."

Chapter 8: A Community in Mourning – Healing from the Trauma

8.1 UAB Hospital: Treating the Physical Wounds

In the hours following the shooting, UAB Hospital became the center of the city's efforts to save lives. Doctors, nurses, and staff worked tirelessly to treat the 18 wounded individuals who had been brought in, some with life-threatening injuries. The emergency room was overwhelmed, but the medical staff's quick actions saved many lives.

8.2 Psychological and Emotional Scars: Mental Health Impacts

For the survivors of the Five Points South shooting, the physical wounds will heal with time. But the psychological scars may last a lifetime. Many of those who were there that night report experiencing flashbacks, nightmares, and severe anxiety. The trauma of surviving a mass shooting can lead to long-term mental health challenges, and many survivors will need ongoing therapy and support.

The mental health impacts extend beyond just the survivors. The families of the victims, the first responders who witnessed the carnage, and even the broader Birmingham community are all grappling with the emotional fallout of the attack.

8.3 Community Support and Vigil: Coming Together After Tragedy

In times of tragedy, communities often come together to support one another, and Birmingham is no different. In the days following the shooting, candlelight vigils were held in Five Points South and across the city. Hundreds of people gathered to mourn the lives lost and to stand in solidarity with the survivors.

Local leaders have called for peace and healing, urging the community to come together in the face of such violence. "We are stronger together," said Birmingham Mayor Randall Woodfin. "This tragedy does not define us—we define how we move forward from here."

Chapter 9: Moving Forward – Lessons for the Future

9.1 Policy Changes and Legislative Proposals

In the wake of the Five Points South shooting, there have been renewed calls for legislative action to prevent similar tragedies from occurring in the future. Alabama lawmakers, including Rep. Phillip Ensler, are once again pushing for stricter gun control measures, including a ban on Glock switches and other firearm modifications that turn guns into fully automatic weapons.

Additionally, there are efforts to increase funding for community programs aimed at reducing gun violence. Some leaders are advocating for more investment in mental health services, education, and job training programs—key factors in addressing the root causes of violence.

9.2 How Communities Can Strengthen Safety

While legislative changes are important, community-led initiatives are also essential in preventing future shootings. Neighborhoods in Birmingham are banding together to create safer environments, from neighborhood watch programs to youth outreach initiatives. Local organizations are working to provide at-risk youth with alternatives to violence, offering mentorship, education, and job training.

Local businesses, too, are playing a role. Many establishments in Five Points South have increased security measures, installing more surveillance cameras and working closely with law enforcement to ensure their patrons are safe.

9.3 A Call for Healing: Moving Forward as One
The path to healing for Birmingham will be long and difficult, but it is possible. The resilience of the community is evident in the way people have come together in the wake of the tragedy. The victims may be gone, but they will not be forgotten, and their memory will fuel the fight to make Birmingham a safer, more just city.

As Birmingham looks to the future, it must confront the challenges that led to this tragedy, from gun violence to systemic inequality. Only by addressing these root causes can the city hope to prevent future tragedies and build a community where everyone feels safe.

Conclusion: The Road Ahead for Birmingham – Healing, Justice, and Prevention

The Five Points South shooting was a devastating reminder of the fragility of life and the dangers that lurk in our communities. But it was also a wake-up call—a stark reminder that gun violence is an epidemic that must be addressed with urgency and compassion.

As Birmingham mourns the lives lost and supports the survivors, the city must also look to the future. Legislative changes, community-led initiatives, and increased support for mental health services are all critical steps in preventing future tragedies. But above all, Birmingham must come together as a community—healing its wounds and standing firm in its resolve to create a safer, more just future for all.